A CHRISTMAS TREASURY

by
Monica Peterson

SANTA MONICA PRESS
P.O. Box 1076
Santa Monica, CA 90406-1076
Printed in the United States
All Rights Reserved

TABLE OF CONTENTS

BIBLICAL ACCOUNTS OF THE BIRTH AND INFANCY OF CHRIST

Saint Matthew

Now the birth of Jesus Christ was on this wise: when as his mother Mary was espoused to Joseph, before they came together, she was found with child of the Holy Ghost. Then Joseph her husband, being a just man, and not willing to make her a public example, was minded to put her away privily. But while he thought on these things, behold the angel of the Lord appeared unto him in a dream, saying, "Joseph, thou son of David, fear not to take unto thee Mary thy wife: for that which is conceived in her is of the Holy Ghost. And she shall bring forth a son, and thou shalt call his name JESUS: for he shall save his people from their sins."

Now all this was done, that it might be fulfilled which was spoken of the Lord by the prophet, saying, "Behold, a virgin shall be with child, and shall bring forth a son, and they shall call his name Emmanuel, which being interpreted is, God with us."

Then Joseph being raised from sleep did as the angel of the Lord had bidden him, and took unto him his wife: and knew her not till she had brought forth her first-born son: and he called his name JESUS.

Now when Jesus was born in Bethlehem of Judea in the days of Herod the king, behold, there came wise men from the east to Jerusalem, saying, "Where is he that is born King of the Jews?

for we have seen his star in the east, and are come to worship him." When Herod the king had heard these things, he was troubled, and all Jerusalem with him. And when he had gathered all the chief priests and scribes of the people together, he demanded of them where Christ should be born. And they said unto him, "In Bethlehem of Judea, for thus it is written by the prophet: 'And thou Bethlehem, in the land of Judah, art not the least among the princes of Judah, for out of thee shall come a governor that shall rule my people Israel.'"

Then Herod, when he had privily called the wise men, inquired of them diligently what time the star appeared. And he sent them to Bethlehem, and said, "Go and search diligently for the young child; and when ye have found him, bring me word again, that I may come and worship him also."

When they had heard the king, they departed; and, lo, the star, which they saw in the east, went before them, till it came and stood over where the young child was. When they saw the star, they rejoiced with exceeding great joy.

And when they were come into the house, they saw the young child with Mary his mother, and fell down, and worshiped him; and when they had opened their treasures, they presented unto him gifts: gold, and frankincense, and myrrh. And being warned of God in a dream that they should not return to Herod, they departed into their own country another way.

And when they were departed, behold, the angel of the Lord appeared to Joseph in a dream, saying, "Arise, and take the young child and his mother, and flee into Egypt, and be thou there until I bring thee word; for Herod will seek the young child to destroy him." When he arose, he took the young child and his mother by night, and departed into Egypt, and was there until the death of Herod, that it might be fulfilled which was spoken of the Lord by the prophet, saying, "Out of Egypt have I called my son."

Then Herod, when he saw that he was mocked of the wise men, was exceeding wroth, and sent forth, and slew all the children that were in Bethlehem, and in all the coasts thereof, from two years old and under, according to the time which he had diligently inquired of the wise men. Then was fulfilled that which was spoken by Jeremiah the prophet, saying, "In Ramah was there a voice heard, lamentation, and weeping, and great mourning, Rachel weeping for her children, and would not be comforted, because they are not."

But when Herod was dead, behold, an angel of the Lord appeareth in a dream to Joseph in Egypt, saying, "Arise, and take the young child and his mother, and go into the land of Israel; for they are dead which sought the young child's life." And he arose, and took the young child and his mother, and came into the land of Israel. But when he heard that Archelaus did reign in Judea in the room of his father Herod, he was afraid to go thither. Notwithstanding, being warned of God in a dream, he turned aside into the parts of Galilee; and he came and dwelt in a city called Nazareth, that it might be fulfilled which was spoken by the prophets, "He shall be called a Nazarene."

Saint Luke

And it came to pass in those days, that there went out a decree from Caesar Augustus, that all the world should be taxed. (And this taxing was first made when Cyrenius was governor of Syria.) And all went to be taxed, every one into his own city. And Joseph also went up from Galilee, out of the city of Nazareth, into Judea, unto the city of David, which is called Bethlehem (because he was of the house and lineage of David), to be taxed with Mary his espoused wife, being great with child.

And so it was, that, while they were there, the days were accomplished that she should be delivered. And she brought forth her first-born son, and wrapped him in swaddling clothes, and laid him in a manger; because there was no room for them in the inn.

And there were in the same country shepherds abiding in the field, keeping watch over their flock by night. And, lo, the angel of the Lord came upon them, and the glory of the Lord shone round about them: and they were sore afraid. And the angel said unto them, "Fear not: for, behold, I bring you good tidings of great joy, which shall be to all people. For unto you is born this day in the city of David a Saviour, which is Christ the Lord. And this shall be a sign unto you: Ye shall find the babe wrapped in swaddling clothes, lying in a manger." And suddenly there was with the angel a multitude of the heavenly host praising God, and saying, "Glory to God in the highest, and on earth peace, good will toward men."

And it came to pass, as the angels were gone away from them into heaven, the shepherds said one to another, "Let us now go even unto Bethlehem, and see this thing which is come to pass, which the Lord hath made known unto us." And they came with haste, and found Mary and Joseph, and the babe lying in the manger. And when they had seen it, they made known abroad the saying which was told them concerning this child. And all they that heard it wondered at those things which were told them by the shepherds. But Mary kept all these things, and pondered them in her heart. And the shepherds returned, glorifying and praising God for all the things that they had heard and seen, as it was told unto them.

CHRISTMAS POEMS

Preparations
Anonymous (Christ Church Manuscript)

Yet if His Majesty, our sovereign lord,
Should of His own accord
Friendly Himself invite,
And say, "I'll be your guest tomorrow night,"
How should we stir ourselves, call and command
All hands to work! "Let no man idle stand!

"Set me fine Spanish tables in the hall;
See they be fitted all;
Let there be room to eat
And order taken that there want no meat.
See every sconce and candlestick made bright,
That without tapers they may give a light.

"Look to the presence: are the carpets spread,
The dazie o'er the head,
The cushions in the chairs,
And all the candles lighted on the stairs?
Perfume the chambers, and in any case
Let each man give attendance in his place!"

Thus, if a king were coming, would we do;
And 'twere good reason too;
For 'tis a duteous thing
To show all honor to an earthly king,
And after all our travail and our cost,

14

So he be pleased, to think no labor lost.
But at the coming of the King of Heaven
All's set at six and seven;
We wallow in our sin,
Christ cannot find a chamber in the inn.
We entertain Him always like a stranger,
And, as at first, still lodge Him in the manger.

From *Hamlet*, Act I, Scene I (Marcellus)
William Shakespeare (1564-1616)

Some say that ever 'gainst that season comes
Wherein our Savior's birth is celebrated,
This bird of dawning singeth all night long:
And then, they say, no spirit dare stire abroad;
The nights are wholesome; then no planets strike,
No fairy takes, nor witch hath power to charm;
So hallowed and so gracious is that time.

A Hymn On The Nativity Of My Saviour
Ben Jonson (1573-1637)

I sing the birth was born tonight,
The Author both of life and light.
   The angels so did sound it.
And like the ravish'd shepherds said,
Who saw the light and were afraid,
   Yet search'd and true they found it.

The Son of God, th' eternal King,
That did us all salvation bring,
   And freed the soul from danger,
He whom the whole world could not take,
The word, which heaven and earth did make,
   Was no laid in a manger.

The Father's wisdom willed it so,
The Son's obedience knew no *no*,
   Both wills were in one stature;
And, as that wisdom had decreed,
The word was now made flesh indeed,
   And took on Him our nature.

What comfort by Him do we win,
Who made Himself the price of sin,
   To make us heirs of glory!
To see this Babe all innocence,
A Martyr born in our defence,
   Can man forget the story?

Ode On The Morning Of Christ's Nativity
John Milton (1608-1674)

This is the month and this the happy morn,
Wherein the Son of Heaven's eternal King,
Of wedded maid and virgin mother born,
Our great redemption from above did bring;
For so the holy sages once did sing
That He our deadly forfeit should release,
And with His Father work us a perpetual peace.

Let Us Sing Our Roundelays
George Wither (1588-1667)

So now is come our joyful'st feast;
Let every man be jolly.
Each room with ivy-leaves is dressed,
And every post with holly.
  Tough some churls at our mirth repine
  Round your foreheads garlands twine,
  Drown sorrow in a cup of wine,
And let us all be merry.

Now all our neighbours' chimneys smoke,
And Christmas blocks are burning;
The ovens they with baked meats choke,
And all their spits are turning.
  Without the door let sorrow lie,
  And if for cold it hap to die,
  We'll bury't in a Christmas pie,
And evermore be merry.

Now every lad is wondrous trim,
And no man minds his labour;
Our lasses have provided them
A bagpipe and a tabor.
  Young men, and maids, and girls and boys,
  Give life to one another's joys,
  And you anon shall by their noise.
Perceive that they are merry.

Then wherefore in these merry days
Should we, I pray, be duller?
No; let us sing our roundelays
To make our mirth the fuller.
   And, whilst thus inspired we sing,
   Let all the streets with echoes ring;
   Woods, and hills, and everything,
Bear witness we are merry.

What Sweeter Music
Robert Herrick (1591-1674)

What sweeter music can we bring
Than a carol for to sing
The birth of this our heavenly King?
Awake the voice! awake the string!
Heart, ear, and eye, and every thing.
Awake! the while the active finger
Runs division with the singer.

Dark and dull night, fly hence away,
And give the honor to this day
That sees December turned to May.

If we ask the reason, say
The why and wherefore all things here
Seem like the springtime of the year.

Why does the chilling winter morn
Smile like a field beset with corn,
Or smell like to a mead new shorn,
Thus on the sudden? Come and see
The cause why things thus fragrant be:
'Tis He is born, whose quick'ning birth
Gives life and luster, public mirth
To heaven, and the under earth.

We see Him come, and know Him ours,
Who with His sunshine and His showers
Turns all the patient ground to flowers.

The Darling of the world is come,
And fit it is we find a room
To welcome Him. The nobler part
Of all the house here is the heart,
Which we will give Him, and bequeath
This holly and this ivy wreath,
To do Him honor, who's our King,
And Lord of all this revelling.

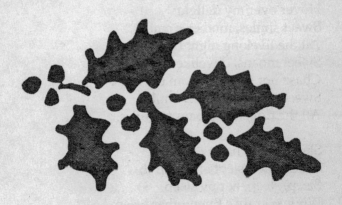

A Cradle Song
William Blake (1757-1827)

Sweet dreams, for a shade
O'er my lovely infant's head;
Sweet dreams of pleasant streams
By happy, silent, moony beams.

Sweet sleep, with soft down
Weave thy brows and infant crown.
Sweet sleep, Angel mild,
Hover o'er my happy child.

Sweet smiles, in the night
Hover over my delight;
Sweet smiles, mother's smiles,
All the livelong night beguiles.
Sweet moans, dovelike sighs,
Chase not slumber from thy eyes.
Sweet moans, sweeter smiles,
All the dovelike moans beguiles.

Sleep, sleep, happy child,
All creation slept and smil'd;
Sleep, sleep, happy sleep,
While o'er thee thy mother weep.
Sweet babe, in thy face
Holy image I can trace.
Sweet babe, once like thee,

Thy Maker lay and wept for me,
Wept for me, for thee, for all,
When He was an infant small.
Thou His image ever see,
Heavenly face that smiles on thee,

Smiles on thee, on me, on all;
Who became an infant small.
Infant smiles are His own smiles;
Heaven and earth to peace beguiles.

A Visit From St. Nicholas
Clement Clarke Moore (1779-1863)

'Twas the night before Christmas, when all
   through the house
Not a creature was stirring, not even a mouse.
The stockings were hung by the chimney with care,
In hopes that St. Nicholas soon would be there.
The children were nestled all snug in their beds,
While visions of sugar-plums danced in their heads;
And mamma in her kerchief, and I in my cap,
Had just settled our brains for a long winter's nap—
When out on the lawn there arose such a clatter
I sprang from my bed to see what was the matter.
Away to the window I flew like a flash,
Tore open the shutter, and threw up the sash.
The moon on the breast of the new-fallen snow
Gave a lustre of midday to objects below;
When what to my wondering eyes should appear
But a miniature sleigh and eight tiny reindeer,
With a little old driver, so lively and quick,
I knew in a moment it must be St. Nick!
More rapid than eagles his coursers they came,
And he whistled and shouted and called them
   by name.
"Now, Dasher! now, Dancer! now, Prancer and Vixen!
On, Comet! on, Cupid! on, Donder and Blitzen!—
To the top of the porch, to the top of the wall,
Now, dash away, dash away, dash away all!"
As dry leaves that before the wild hurricane fly,

When they meet with an obstacle mount to the sky,
So, up to the housetop the coursers they flew,
With a sleigh full of toys—and St. Nicholas, too.
And then, in a twinkling, I heard on the roof
The prancing and pawing of each little hoof.
As I drew in my head and was turning around,
Down the chimney St. Nicholas came with a bound:
He was dressed all in fur from his head to his foot,
And his clothes were all tarnished with ashes and soot:
A bundle of toys he had flung on his back,
And he looked like a peddler just opening his pack.
His eyes, how they twinkled! his dimples, how merry!
His cheeks were like roses, his nose like a cherry;
His droll little mouth was drawn up like a bow,
And the bard on his chin was as white as the snow.
The stump of a pipe he held tight in his teeth,
And the smoke, it encircled his head like a wreath.
He had a broad face and a little round belly
That shook, when he laughed, like a bowl full of jelly.
He was chubby and plump—a right jolly old elf:
And I laughed when I saw him, in spite of myself;
A wink of his eye, and a twist of his head,
Soon gave me to know I had nothing to dread.
He spoke not a word, but went straight to his work,
And filled all the stockings: then turned with a jerk,
And laying his finger aside of his nose,
And giving a nod, up the chimney he rose.
He sprang to his sleigh, to his team gave a whistle,
And away they all flew like the down of a thistle.
But I heard him exclaim, ere they drove out of sight,
"Happy Christmas to all, and to all a good-night!"

25

The Three Kings
Henry Wadsworth Longfellow (1807-1882)

Three Kings came riding from far away,
  Melchior and Gaspar and Baltasar;
Three Wise Men out of the East were they,
And they traveled by night and they slept by day,
  For their guide was a beautiful, wonderful star.

The star was so beautiful, large and clear,
  That all the other stars of the sky
Became a white mist in the atmosphere;
And by this they knew that the coming was near
  Of the Prince foretold in the prophecy.

Three caskets they bore on their saddle-bows,
  Three caskets of gold with golden keys;
Their robes were of crimson silk, with rows
Of bells and pomegranates and furbelows,
  Their turbans like blossoming almond-trees.

And so the Three Kings rode into the West,
  Through the dusk of night over hill and dell,
And sometimes they nodded with beard on breast,
And sometimes talked, as they paused to rest,
  With the people they met at some wayside well.

"Of the Child that is born," said Baltasar,
  "Good people, I pray you, tell us the news;

For we in the East have seen His star,
And have ridden fast, and have ridden far,
  To find and worship the King of the Jews."

And the people answered, "You ask in vain;
  We know of no king but Herod the Great!"
They thought the Wise Men were men insane,
As they spurred their horses across the plain
  Like riders in haste who cannot wait.

And when they came to Jerusalem,
  Herod the Great, who had heard this thing,
Sent for the Wise Men and questioned them;
And said, "Go down unto Bethlehem,
  And bring me tidings of this new king."

So they rode away, and the star stood still,
  The only one in the gray of morn;
Yes, it stopped, it stood still of its own free will,
Right over Bethlehem on the hill,
  The city of David where Christ was born.

And the Three Kings rode through the gate and
  the guard,
  Through the silent street, till their horses turned
And neighed as they entered the great inn-yard;
But the windows were closed, and the doors were
  barred,
  And only a light in the stable burned.

27

And cradled there in the scented hay,
  In the air made sweet by the breath of kine,
The little Child in the manger lay,
The Child that would be King one day
  Of a kingdom not human, but divine.

His mother, Mary of Nazareth,
  Sat watching beside his place of rest,
Watching the even flow of his breath,
For the joy of life and the terror of death
  Were mingled together in her breast.

They laid their offerings at his feet:
  The gold was their tribute to a King;
The frankincense, with its odor sweet,
Was for the Priest, the Paraclete;
  The myrrh for the body's burying.

And the mother wondered and bowed her head,
  And sat as still as a stature of stone;
Her heart was troubled yet comforted,
Remembering what the angel had said
  Of an endless reign and of David's throne.

Then the Kings rode out of the city gate,
  With a clatter of hoofs in proud array;
But they went not back to Herod the Great,
For they knew his malice and feared his hate,
  And returned to their homes by another way.

My Gift
Christina G. Rossetti (1830-1894)

What can I give Him
Poor as I am;
If I were a shepherd,
I would give Him a lamb.
If I were a wise man,
I would do my part.
But what can I give Him?
I will give Him my heart.

A Christmas Hymn
Christina G. Rossetti (1830-1894)

Love came down at Christmas,
Love all lovely, Love Divine;
Love was born at Christmas,
Star and Angels gave the sign.

Worship we the Godhead,
Love incarnate, Love Divine;
Worship we our Jesus:
But wherewith for sacred sign?

Love shall be our token,
Love be yours and love be mine,
Love to God and all men,
Love for plea and gift and sign.

Heaven Cannot Hold Him
Christina Rossetti (1830-1894)

In the bleak midwinter
  Frosty wind made moan,
Earth stood hard as iron,
  Water like a stone;
Snow had fallen, snow on snow,
  Snow on snow,
In the bleak midwinter
  Long ago.

Our God, Heaven cannot hold Him
  Nor earth sustain;
Heaven and earth shall flee away
  When He comes to reign:
In the bleak midwinter
  A stable-place sufficed
The Lord God Almighty
  Jesus Christ.

Enough for Him, whom cherubim
  Worship night and day,
A breastful of milk
  And a mangerful of hay;
Enough for Him, whom angels
  Fall down before,
The ox and ass and camel
  Which adore.

Angels and archangels
　　May have gathered there,
Cherubim and seraphim
　　Thronged the air;
But only His mother
　　In her maiden bliss
Worshipped the Beloved
　　With a kiss.

What can I give Him,
　　Poor as I am?
If I were a shepherd
　　I would bring a lamb,
If I were a Wise Man
　　I would do my part,—
Yet what I can I give Him,
　　Give my heart.

Signs Of Christmas

William Hone's Year Book, 1832

When on the barn's thatch'd roof is seen
The moss in tufts of liveliest green;
When Roger to the woodpile goes,
And, as he turns, his fingers blows;
When all around is cold and drear,
Be sure that Christmastide is near.

When up the garden walk in vain
We seek for Flora's lovely train;
When the sweet hawthorn bower is bare,
And bleak and cheerless is the air;
When all seems desolate around,
Christmas advances o'er the ground.

When Tom at eve comes home from plough,
And brings the mistletoe's green bough,
With the milk-white berries spotted o'er,
And shakes it the sly maids before,
Then hangs the trophy up on high,
Be sure that Christmastide is nigh.

When Hal, the woodman, in his clogs
Brings home the huge unwieldy logs,
That, hissing on the smould'ring fire,
Flame out at last a quivering spire;
When in his hat the holly stands,
Old Christmas musters up his bands.

When, clustered round the fire at night,
Old William talks of ghost and sprite,
And, as a distant outhouse gate
Slams by the wind, they fearful wait,
While some each shadowy nook explore,
Then Christmas pauses at the door.

When Dick comes shiv'ring from the yard,
And says, "The pond is frozen hard,"
While from his cap, all white with snow,
The moisture trickling drops below;
While carols sound, the night to cheer,
Then Christmas and his train are here.

Christmas-Greetings
From A Fairy To A Child
Lewis Carroll (1832-1898)

Lady, dear, if Fairies may
For a moment lay aside
Cunning tricks and elfish play,
'Tis at happy Christmas-tide.

We have heard the children say —
Gentle children, whom we love —
Long ago, on Christmas Day,
Came a message from above.

Still, as Christmas-tide comes round,
They remember it again—
Echo still the joyful sound
"Peace on earth, good-will to men!"

Yet the hearts must childlike be
Where such heavenly guests abide;
Unto children, in their glee,
All the year is Christmas-tide!

Thus, forgetting tricks and play
For a moment, Lady dear,
We would wish you, if we may
Merry Christmas, glad New Year!

A Christmas Prayer
Robert Louis Stevenson (1850-1894)

Loving Father, help us remember the birth of Jesus, that we may share in the song of the angels, the gladness of the shepherds, and the worship of the wise men.

Close the door of hate and open the door of love all over the world.

Let kindness come with every gift and good desires with every greeting.

Deliver us from evil by the blessing which Christ brings, and teach us to be merry with clear hearts.

May the Christmas morning make us happy to be Thy children, and the Christmas evening bring us to our beds with grateful thoughts, forgiving and forgiven, for Jesus' sake. Amen!

CHRISTMAS CAROLS

The Holly And The Ivy
Traditional (15th Century)

The Holly and the Ivy,
  When they are both full grown
Of all the trees are in the wood,
  The Holly bears the crown.

O the rising of the sun,
  And the running of the deer,
The playing of the merry organ,
  Sweet singing in the choir.

The Holly bears a blossom
  As white as any flower;
And Mary bore sweet Jesus Christ
  To be our sweet Saviour.

The Holly bears a berry
  As red as any blood;
And Mary bore sweet Jesus Christ
  To do poor sinners good.

The Holly bears a prickle
  As sharp as any thorn;
And Mary bore sweet Jesus Christ
  On Christmas in the morn.

The Holly bears a bark
  As bitter as any gall;
And Mary bore sweet Jesus Christ
  For to redeem us all.

The Holly and the Ivy
  Now both are full well grown:
Of all the trees are in the wood
  The Holly bears the crown.

Carol
Traditional (15th century)

I sing of a maiden
  That is matchless;
King of all kings
  To her Son she chose.

He came all so still
  There His mother was,
As dew in April
  That falleth on the grass.

He came all so still
  To His mother's bower,
As dew in April
  That falleth on the flower.

He came all so still
  There His mother lay,
As dew in April
  That falleth on the spray.

Mother and maiden
  Was never none but she;
Well may such a lady
  Godde's mother be.

Angels We Have Heard On High
Traditional (15th Century)

Angels we have heard on high,
Sweetly singing o'er our plains,
And the mountains in reply
Echoing their joyous strains.
Gloria in excelsis Deo, Gloria in excelsis Deo.

In the fields, beside their sheep,
Shepherds watching thro' the night,
Hear, amid the silence deep,
Those sweet voices, clear and bright.
Gloria in excelsis Deo, Gloria in excelsis Deo.

Joyful hearts with one accord,
Spread the tidings far and wide:
Born to us is Christ the Lord,
At this happy Christmas tide.
Gloria in excelsis Deo, Gloria in excelsis Deo.

O Christmas Tree
Traditional

O Christmas tree, O Christmas tree,
With faithful leaves unchanging;
Not only green in summer's heat,
But also winter's snow and sleet,
O Christmas tree, O Christmas tree
With faithful leaves unchanging.

O Christmas tree, O Christmas tree,
Of all the trees most lovely;
Each year, you bring to me delight
Gleaming in the Christmas night.
O Christmas tree, O Christmas tree,
Of all the trees most lovely.

O Christmas tree, O Christmas tree,
Your leaves will teach me also,
That hope and love and faithfulness
Are precious things I can possess.
O Christmas tree, O Christmas tree,
Your leaves will teach me, also.

Gloucestershire Wassail
Traditional (18th Century)

Wassail, wassail, all over the town;
 Our bread it is white and our ale it is brown.
Our bowl it is made of the white maple tree:
 With the wass'ling bowl we'll drink unto Thee!

Then here's to the horse, and to his right eye!
 May God send our master a good Christmas pie,
A good Christmas pie that may we all see!
 With the wass'ling bowl we'll drink unto Thee!

Then here's to the ox, and to his long tail!
 Pray God send our master a bowl of strong ale,
A bowl of strong ale that may we all see!
 With the wass'ling bowl we'll drink unto Thee!

Come, butler, come fill us a bowl of the best!
 Then we hope that your soul in heaven may rest.
But if you do draw us a bowl of the small,
 May the devil take butler, bowl, and all!

Then here's to the maid in the lily white smock,
 Who tripp'd to the door and slipp'd back the lock,
Who tripp'd to the door and pull'd back the pin.
 For to let these jolly wassailers walk in.

Wassail, wassail all over the town;
 Our bread it is white and our ale it is brown
Our bowl it is made of the white maple tree!
 With the wass'ling bowl we'll drink to Thee!

While Shepherds Watched Their Flocks By Night
Nahum Tate (1652-1715)

While shepherds watched their flocks by night,
All seated on the ground,
The angel of the Lord came down,
And glory shone around, and glory shone around.

"To you, in David's town this day,
Is born of David's line,
The Saviour, who is Christ, the Lord,
And this shall be the sign: and this shall be the sign:

"The heav'nly babe you there shall find
To human view displayed,
All meanly wrapped in swathing bands,
and in a manger laid. And in a manger laid."

Thus spake the seraph—and forthwith
appeared a shining throng
Of angels, praising God, who thus
Addressed their joyful song; addressed their
  joyful song;

"All glory be to God on high,
And to the earth be peace;
Good will henceforth from heaven to men
Begin, and never cease! Begin and never cease!"

Joy To The World
Issac Watts (1674-1748)

Joy to the world! the Lord is come:
  Let earth receive her King;
Let every heart prepare Him room,
  And heaven and nature sing, and heaven and
  nature sing.

Joy to the earth! the Saviour reigns:
  Let men their songs employ,
While fields and floods, rocks, hills, and plains
  Repeat the sounding joy, repeat the sounding joy.

No more let sins and sorrows grow,
  Nor thorns infest the ground;
He comes to make His blessings flow
  As far as sin is found, as far as sin is found.
He rules the world with truth and grace,
  And makes the nations prove
The glories of His righteousness,
  And wonders of His love, and wonders of His love.

The First Noel
Traditional (17th Century)

The first Noel the angel did say
Was to certain poor shepherds, in fields as they lay;
In fields where they lay, keeping their sheep.
On a cold winter's night that was so deep.

Noel, noel, noel, noel!
Born is the King of Israel.

They looked up and saw a star,
Shining in the east beyond them far,
And to the earth it gave great light,
And so it continued both day and night.

Noel, noel, noel, noel!
Born is the King of Israel.

And by the light of that same star,
Three wise men came from country far;
To seek for a king was their intent,
And to follow the star wherever it went.

Noel, noel, noel, noel!
Born is the King of Israel.

This star drew nigh to the northwest,
O'er Bethlehem it took its rest,
And there it did both stop and stay,
Right o'er the place where Jesus lay.

Noel, noel, noel, noel!
Born is the King of Israel.

Then did they know assuredly,
Within that house the King did lie;
One entered in then for to see,
And found the Babe in poverty.

Noel, noel, noel, noel!
Born is the King of Israel.

Then entered in those wise men three,
Most reverently upon their knee,
And offered there, in His presence,
Their gold, and myrrh, and frankincense.

Noel, noel, noel, noel!
Born is the King of Israel.

Between an ox-stall and an ass
This Child truly there born He was;
For want of clothing they did Him lay
All in the manger, among the hay.

Noel, noel, noel, noel!
Born is the King of Israel.

Then let us all with one accord,
Sing praises to our Heavenly Lord,
That hath made Heaven and earth of naught,
And with His blood mankind hath bought.

Noel, noel, noel, noel!
Born is the King of Israel.

If we in our time shall do well,
We shall be free from death and hell;
For God hath prepared for us all
A resting-place in general.

Noel, noel, noel, noel!
Born is the King of Israel.

God Rest You Merry, Gentlemen
Traditional (18th Century)

God rest you merry, gentlemen,
  Let nothing you dismay,
Remember Christ, our Saviour
  Was born on Christmas Day,
To save us all from Satan's power
  When we were gone astray.

O tidings of comfort and joy,
Comfort and joy,
O tidings of comfort and joy.

In Bethlehem, in Jewry,
  This blessed Babe was born.
And laid within a manger,
  Upon this blessed morn;
The which His Mother Mary,
  Did nothing take in scorn

Chorus

Now to the Lord sing praises,
  All you within this place,
And with true love and brotherhood
  Each other now embrace;
This holy tide of Christmas
  All other doth deface.

Chorus

Deck The Halls
Traditional

Deck the halls with boughs of holly,
Fa la la la la la la la la.
'Tis the season to be jolly,
Fa la la la la la la la la.
Don we now our gay apparel,
Fa la la la la la la la la.
Troll the ancient yuletide carol,
Fa la la la la la la la la.

See the blazing yule before us,
Fa la la la la la la la la.
Strike the harp and join the chorus,
Fa la la la la la la la la.
Follow me in merry measure,
Fa la la la la la la la la.
While I tell you of yuletide treasure,
Fa la la la la la la la la.

Fast away the old year passes,
Fa la la la la la la la la.
Hail the new, ye lads and lassies,
Fa la la la la la la la la.
Sing we joyous all together,
Fa la la la la la la la la.
Heedless of the wind and weather,
Fa la la la la la la la la.

Go Tell It On The Mountain
Traditional Spiritual

Go tell it on the mountain,
Over the hills and everywhere;
Go tell it on the mountain,
That Jesus Christ is born.

　When I was a seeker,
　I sought both night and day,
　I asked the Lord to help me,
　And He showed me the way.

　He made me a watchman
　Upon a city wall,
　And if I am a Christian,
　I am the least of all.

Go tell it on the mountain,
Over the hills and everywhere;
Go tell it on the mountain,
That Jesus Christ is born.

Here We Come A'Wassailing
Traditional

Here we come a'wassailing
  Among the leaves so green,
Here we come a'wand'ring
  So fair to be seen.

Love and joy come to you,
And to you, your wassail too,
And God bless you, and send you
A happy New Year,
And God send you a happy New Year

We are not daily beggars
  That beg from door to door,
But we are neighbour's children
  Whom you have seen before

Chorus

Good Master and good Mistress
  As you sit by the fire,
Pray think of us poor children
  Who are wandering in the mire.

Chorus

We have a little purse
 Made of ratching leather skin;
We want some of your small change
 To line it well within.

Chorus

Bring us out a table,
 And spread it with a cloth;
Bring us out a mouldy cheese,
 And some of your Christmas loaf.

Chorus

God bless the master of this house,
 Likewise the mistress too;
And all the little children
 That round the table go.

Chorus

53

The Twelve Days Of Christmas
Traditional

On the first day of Christmas
My true love sent to me
A partridge in a pear tree.

On the second day of Christmas
My true love sent to me
Two turtle doves, and
A partridge in a pear tree.

On the third day of Christmas
My true love sent to me
Three French hens,
Two turtle doves, and
A partridge in a pear tree.

On the fourth day of Christmas
My true love sent to me
Four colly birds,
Three French hens,
Two turtle doves, and
A partridge in a pear tree.

On the fifth day of Christmas
My true love sent to me
Five gold rings,
Four colly birds,

Three French hens,
Two turtle doves, and
A partridge in a pear tree.

On the sixth day of Christmas
My true love sent to me
Six geese a-laying,
Five gold rings,
Four colly birds,
Three French hens,
Two turtle doves, and
A partridge in a pear tree.

On the seventh day of Christmas
My true love sent to me
Seven swans a-swimming,
Six geese a-laying,
Five gold rings,
Four colly birds,
Three French hens,
Two turtle doves, and
A partridge in a pear tree.

On the eighth day of Christmas
My true love sent to me
Eight maids a-milking,
Seven swans a-swimming,
Six geese a-laying,
Five gold rings,

Four colly birds,
Three French hens,
Two turtle doves, and
A partridge in a pear tree.

On the ninth day of Christmas
My true love sent to me
Nine ladies dancing,
Eight maids a-milking,
Seven swans a-swimming,
Six geese a-laying,
Five gold rings,
Four colly birds,
Three French hens,
Two turtle doves, and
A partridge in a pear tree.

On the tenth day of Christmas
My true love sent to me
Ten lords a-leaping,
Nine ladies dancing,
Eight maids a-milking,
Seven swans a-swimming,
Six geese a-laying,
Five gold rings,
Four colly birds,
Three French hens,
Two turtle doves, and
A partridge in a pear tree.

On the eleventh day of Christmas
My true love sent to me
Eleven drummers drumming,
Ten lords a-leaping,
Nine ladies dancing,
Eight maids a-milking,
Seven swans a-swimming,
Six geese a-laying,
Five gold rings,
Four colly birds,
Three French hens,
Two turtle doves, and
A partridge in a pear tree.

On the twelfth day of Christmas
My true love sent to me
Twelve pipers piping,
Eleven drummers drumming,
Ten lords a-leaping,
Nine ladies dancing,
Eight maids a-milking,
Seven swans a-swimming,
Six geese a-laying,
Five gold rings,
Four colly birds,
Three French hens,
Two turtle doves, and
A partridge in a pear tree.

O Come, All Ye Faithful
Traditional (18th Century)

O come, all ye faithful, joyful and triumphant,
O come ye, O come ye to Bethlehem;
Come and behold Him, born the King of angels;
O come, let us adore Him, O come, let us adore Him,
O come, let us adore Him, Christ the Lord.

Lo, humble shepherds, hasting to His cradle,
Leaving their flocks in the fields, draw near.
We, too, with gladness, thither bend our footsteps,
O come, let us adore Him, O come, let us adore Him,
O come, let us adore Him, Christ the Lord.

Sing, choirs of angels, sing in exultation,
Sing, all ye citizens of heav'n above:
"Glory to God in the highest";
O come, let us adore Him, O come, let us adore Him,
O come, let us adore Him, Christ the Lord.

Silent Night
Joseph Mohr (1792-1848)

Silent night! Holy night!
All is calm, all is bright;
Round yon virgin mother and Child,
Holy Infant so tender and mild;
Sleep in heavenly peace,
Sleep in heavenly peace.

Silent night! Holy night!
Darkness flies, all is light;
Shepherds hear the angels sing:
"Alleluia! hail the King!
Christ the Saviour is born,
Christ the Saviour is born."

Silent night! Holy night!
Guiding Star, lend thy light!
See the eastern wise men bring
Gifts and homage to our King!
Christ the Saviour is born,
Christ the Saviour is born.

Silent night! Holy night!
Wondrous Star, lend thy light!
With the angels let us sing
Alleluia to our King!
Christ the Saviour is born,
Christ the Saviour is born.

I Heard The Bells On Christmas Day
Henry Wadsworth Longfellow (1807-1882)

I heard the bells on Christmas day
Their old, familiar carols play,
  And wild and sweet
  The words repeat
Of peace on earth, good-will to men!

And thought how, as the day had come,
The belfries of all Christendom
  Had rolled along
  The unbroken song,
Of peace on earth, good-will to men!

Till, ringing, swinging on its way,
The world revolved from night to day,
  A voice, a chime,
  A chant sublime
Of peace on earth, good-will to men!

Then from each black, accursed mouth
The cannon thundered in the South,
  And with the sound
  The carols drowned
Of peace on earth, good-will to men!

It was as if an earthquake rent
The hearth-stones of a continent,
   And made forlorn
   The households born
Of peace on earth, good-will to men!

And in despair I bowed my head;
"There is no peace on earth," I said;
   "For hate is strong,
   And mocks the song
Of peace on earth, good-will to men!"

Then pealed the bells more loud and deep:
"God is not dead; nor doth He sleep!
   The Wrong shall fail,
   The Right prevail,
With peace on earth, good-will to men!"

61

It Came Upon The Midnight Clear
Edmund Hamilton Sears (1810-1876)

It came upon the midnight clear,
   That glorious song of old,
From angels bending near the earth,
   To touch their harps of gold;
"Peace on the earth, good will to men,
   From heav'n's all-gracious King."
The world in solemn stillness lay
   To hear the angels sing.

Still thro' the cloven skies they come,
   With peaceful wings unfurled;
And still their heavenly music floats
   O'er all the weary world:
Above its sad and lowly plains
   They bend on hovering wing,
And ever o'er its Babel sounds
   The blessed angels sing.

But with the woes of sin and strife
   The world has suffered long;
Beneath the angel-strain have rolled
   Two thousand years of wrong;
And man, at war with man, hears not
   The love song which they bring;
O hush the noise, ye men of strife,
   And hear the angels sing!

And ye, beneath life's crushing load
    Whose forms are bending low,
Who toil along the climbing way,
    With painful steps and slow—
Look now; for glad and golden hours
    Come swiftly on the wing:
O rest beside the weary road,
    And hear the angels sing!

We Three Kings Of Orient Are
John H. Hopkins, Jr., (1820-1891)

We three kings of Orient are;
Bearing gifts we traverse afar
Field and fountain, moor and mountain,
Following yonder star.

O star of wonder, star of might, star, with royal
   beauty bright,
Westward leading, still proceeding, guide us to
   thy perfect light.

Born a King on Bethlehem's plain,
Gold I bring, to crown Him again,
King forever, ceasing never,
Over us all to reign.

O star of wonder, star of might, star, with royal
   beauty bright,
Westward leading, still proceeding, guide us to
   thy perfect light.

Frankincense to offer have I,
Incense owns a Deity nigh.
Prayer and praising, all men raising,
Worship God most high.

O star of wonder, star of might, star, with royal
    beauty bright,
Westward leading, still proceeding, guide us to
    thy perfect light.

Myrrh is mine, its bitter perfume
Breathes a life of gathering gloom;
Sorrowing, sighing, bleeding, dying,
Sealed in the stone-cold tomb.

O star of wonder, star of might, star, with royal
    beauty bright,
Westward leading, still proceeding, guide us to
    thy perfect light.

See Him now in power arise,
Might through His sacrifice.
Alleluia! Alleluia!
Echo it, earth and skies.

O star of wonder, star of might, star, with royal
    beauty bright,
Westward leading, still proceeding, guide us to
    thy perfect light.

O Little Town Of Bethlehem
Phillips Brooks (1868-1893)

O little town of Bethlehem,
  How still we see thee lie!
Above thy deep and dreamless sleep
  The silent stars go by;
Yet in thy dark streets shineth
  The everlasting light;
The hopes and fears of all the years
  Are met in thee tonight

For Christ is born of Mary;
  And, gather'd all above,
While mortals sleep, the angels keep
  Their watch of wond'ring love.
O morning stars, together
  Proclaim the holy birth!
And praises sing to God, the King,
  And peace to men on earth.

How silently, how silently,
  The wondrous gift is given!
So God imparts to human hearts
  The blessings of His heaven.
No ear may hear His coming,
  But in this world of sin,
Where meek souls will receive Him still,
  The dear Christeners in.

O holy Child of Bethlehem!
  Descend to us, we pray;
Cast out our sin and enter in,
  Be born in us today.
We hear the Christmas angels,
  The great glad tidings tell;
O come to us, abide with us,
  Our Lord Immanuel!

Jingle Bells
John Pierpont (1785-1866)

Dashing through the snow,
In a one horse open sleigh;
O'er the fields we go,
Laughing all the way;
Bells on bob tail ring,
Making spirits bright;
Oh what sport to ride and sing
A sleighing song tonight.

Jingle bells, jingle bells,
Jingle all the way;
Oh! What joy it is to ride
In a one horse open sleigh.
Jingle bells, jingle bells,
Jingle all the way.
Oh! What joy it is to ride
In a one horse open sleigh.

THE HISTORY OF CHRISTMAS AND CHRISTMAS TRADITIONS

Christmas

In 337 A.D., the Roman emperor Constantine was baptized, thus uniting the emperorship and the Church. With Christianity as the official state religion, Christmas celebrations began to appear throughout the Western world. However, the date on which the celebrations should occur was in dispute. Despite the fact that Christmas is now celebrated on December 25, that date is not believed to be Christ's actual birthday. Nobody really knows the exact date on which Jesus was born. Some biblical scholars have speculated that his birthday was once celebrated on January 6, and that this holiday was called "the Nativity." Another festival, Epiphany, was also known to be held on that same date at various times throughout our history. The Epiphany was a celebration of Christ's baptism and the Magi's visit to the stable in Bethlehem.

In 354 A.D., Pope Liberius of Rome declared that December 25 should mark the birth of Christ. Because other popular religions of the time, in particular "Mithraism," also celebrated holidays at this time of the year, some scholars have suggested that the Pope chose this date in order to prevent Christians from becoming tempted to join the followers of these other religions, or "pagans," during the pagan festivals that would occur around this time of year.

Among the most popular pagan festivals were the *Natalis Solis Invicti* or "Birthday of the Invincible Sun God" (December 25); *Saturnalia* (December 17 to December 24), and *Kalends* (January 1 to January 4). These celebrations were quite lively, and many of our most beloved Christmas traditions are derived from these ancient festivals. For example, people would give each other gifts, such as holly branches. Work would come to a halt, great feasts were held, and homes were decorated with lights and plants. The pagans used evergreens as a symbol of life during the harsh, cold winter. They believed that the use of such plants as holly, ivy, and mistletoe would help the sun to rise again while at the same time fend off the ghosts and goblins who were thought to sneak into their homes in order to warm themselves. This latter use of plants was a forebearer to our contemporary custom of filling our homes with evergreens during Christmas.

Christmas Cards

The practice of sending Christmas cards is fairly new, perhaps dating back only 150 years or so. In the nineteenth century, British schoolboys began sending handwritten "Christmas pieces" to their parents. This early version of a Christmas card featured painted borders and messages or poems.

While nobody really knows who invented the modern day Christmas card, the oldest known card is owned by Rust Craft Publishers in Dedham, Massachusetts. Made of paper lace, the card says, "A Merry Christmas to You," on the front, and "A Happy Christmas to My Mother Dear, 1839," on the back.

A wealthy British businessman, Sir Henry Cole, is known to have hired London artist John Calcott Horsley in 1843 to illustrate the first Christmas card designed for sale. Horsley created a triptych, with the side panels featuring people "feeding the hungry" and "clothing the naked," and the centerpiece displaying a family celebrating Christmas. Next to the illustration, the words, "A Merry Christmas and a Happy New Year," are written. Cole sold one thousand of these cards, of which twelve remain in existence today.

Christmas cards made their appearance in America in the 1850s, but didn't become universally popular until the 1870s. Louis Prang, a lithographer from Roxbury, Massachusetts, was among the early designers of American Christmas cards, earning him the title, "Father of the American Christmas card." However, Prang's high-quality cards proved to be too expensive for most Americans, and he was out of business by the 1890s, having been replaced by the far cheaper Christmas postcards which were imported from Germany. These so-called penny cards remained popular until World War I, when the modern American greeting card industry sprang into motion. With over two billion cards exchanged every holiday season, Christmas is easily the most popular card-selling time of the year.

Christmas Carols

The word "carol" comes from the Greek word, *choraulein*. A *choraulein* was a Greek dance which was performed in a circle and was accompanied by the flute. The Romans borrowed the tradition of the *choraulein* and eventually brought it to England. The English altered the custom by replacing the flute with singing. They described their new dance as a "carol." Over time, carol became a description of the songs as opposed to the dance.

The songs themselves can be traced back to St. Francis of Assisi and his followers, who were renowned for their gorgeous Christmas hymns. These hymns were eventually spread throughout Europe by strolling singers and musicians known as troubadours. The songs were initially sung in Latin, but by the fifteenth century, English became the dominant language with which the songs were composed. The first English carol, "I Saw a Sweet, Seemly Sight," was written in the early 1400s.

Christmas carols were banned by Oliver Cromwell in the mid-1600s. Cromwell apparently felt that Christmas was a solemn day, and that it was not appropriate to sing carols and attend parties. The British, however, continued to celebrate Christmas with songs and parties behind the backs of their kings and queens, and by the mid-1800s, under Queen Victoria, Christmas celebrations were brought out into the open once again.

Scholars believe that the first American Christmas carols were sung by the Huron Indians. In the seventeenth century, the Hurons would get together, build a manger, and sing hymns around it in honor of the birth of Jesus. In 1908, people began the tradition of singing Christmas carols outside in the streets of Boston. Ditto for St. Louis in 1909, where groups would sing hymns in front of houses which had a candle burning in the window.

The Christmas Crèche

The tradition of setting up the crèche, or model of the manger at Bethlehem, most likely began in Italy. The word *crèche* is French for "manger." The French word is thought to have come from the Italian *Greccio*. Greccio is the Italian town in which a famous crèche was built by St. Francis of Assisi in the thirteenth century. While mangers had been built in churches for hundreds of years before St. Francis came along, they tended to be filled with gold, silver, and jewels. St. Francis realized that it was important that people remembered that Christ was born in a humble stable. Therefore, he built his crèche without the fancy *accoutrements*.

Crèches became popular in America in 1741 when German immigrants in Bethlehem, Pennsylvania brought their version of the crèche, known as *putzes*, with them to the New Country. Other immigrants also brought their own crèches to America, and these lovely scenes are now a beloved Christmas tradition.

Christmas Trees

As with holly, ivy, and mistletoe, Christmas trees were used by pagans for their power as evergreens. However, pagans would only bring branches of these trees into their houses. It wasn't until the eighth century, in Germany, that people began cutting down whole trees and placing them inside of their homes. A British monk named St. Boniface was preaching to a tribe of Germanic Druids near the town of Geismar. Attempting to disabuse them of their belief that the oak tree was sacred, St. Boniface chopped one down. When it fell, the giant oak crushed every plant and tree in its path with the exception of a small fir tree. St. Boniface, taking advantage of the situation, declared that the fir's survival was a miracle and proclaimed, "Let this be called the tree of the Christ Child."

The way in which the custom of decorating Christmas trees got started is not known, although there are many theories. One popular belief is that Martin Luther began the tradition in the fifteenth century. While walking through the woods on Christmas Eve, Martin Luther glanced up at the sky and saw stars sparkling through the branches of a fir tree. In order to replicate the awe-inspiring sight, he cut down the tree, brought it into his home, and placed candles on its branches.

Another theory about the decoration of Christmas trees begins in Germany in the Middle Ages. On December 25, peasants would perform plays about Adam and Eve in front of the local church. The actors would hang apples on the branches of an evergreen to symbolize the tree of good and evil. When Church leaders eventually banned the performance of such plays, people began bringing the so-called "Adam and Eve" trees into their homes on December 25. They would decorate these evergreens and small firs with apples, as well as roses and wafers (which stood for Mary and Jesus). Such decorated trees were known as *Christbaum*, or "Christ tree." By the 1700s, the Germans were placing candles on their *Christbaum*.

Queen Victoria's German husband, Albert, missed the *Christbaum* when he moved to England in the mid-nineteenth century, and in 1841 he began the custom of decorating a Christmas tree in Windsor Castle. The decorating fever caught on, and soon everyone in England was decorating their own tree at Christmas.

Germans are also most likely responsible for the use of decorated Christmas trees in America. In the mid-1700s, German immigrants in Bethlehem, Pennsylvania were known to be decorating Christmas trees. After Thomas Edison invented the electric light bulb in 1879, Americans began experimenting with trimming their trees with electric lights. However, it wasn't until electric lights on strings were invented in 1907 that decorating Christmas trees became a widespread tradition in America.

Holly and Ivy

The early leaders of the Christian Church did not approve of the pagan tradition of bringing evergreens indoors. But the pagans continued to do so, even after they became Christians. In an effort to accommodate their new members, the leaders weaved evergreens into the story of Christ.

They developed the legend that the crown of thorns which Christ wore before his death was made of holly leaves, and that when the crown pricked Christ's forehead, he began to bleed all over the holly berries, which turned from white to red. Once this legend was firmly established and widely accepted, holly became a traditional Christmas decoration.

Ivy took much longer to be accepted by the Christian Church because of its association with the Roman god Bacchus. Because he was the god of wine and was himself associated with drunken revelries, Christian leaders did not want ivy to be a part of their Church. Once again, however, the former pagans prevailed, and their insistence on using ivy as a part of their Christmas celebrations eventually won out over the Christian leader's objections.

Midnight Mass

According to legend, Christ was born at midnight, and we thus attend church at that hour on Christmas. During midnight mass, the church is often lit up by candles in order to symbolize the brightness which Christ brought with him into the world. The practice of ringing midnight chimes dates back to the Middle Ages, when bells were rung repeatedly between eleven o'clock and midnight as a part of the "devil's funeral." It was believed that the devil died when Christ was born, and thus at midnight the bells broke out into sounds of Christmas joy.

Mistletoe

The history of mistletoe actually goes back to the Second Century B.C. and the British Isles, where the Celts and their priests, the Druids, believed that the mistletoe which grew on oak trees had divine power. They would use mistletoe in elaborate sacrificial ceremonies, placing it on the altar with animals they were sacrificing to the gods. After the ceremony, the Druids would give the people pieces of the mistletoe to hang above their doors in order to bring them good luck.

The Druids also believed in the healing powers of mistletoe. Childless women and animals would eat the mistletoe in order to help them get pregnant. Everything from skin diseases to epilepsy was thought to be able to be cured by mistletoe. And if two enemies happened to meet under a tree which bore mistletoe, they were required to lay their arms on the ground and declare a truce for that day.

The custom of kissing under the mistletoe originates from a Scandinavian legend. The god Balder dreamed that he was going to die. His mother Frigga, the goddess of love, was frightened by this dream, and so made every person and every thing on the planet promise not to harm her son. However, she forgot to ask the seemingly harmless mistletoe, or *mistilteinn*. Another god, Loki, was a jealous rival of Balder. He sought out the blind god Hother and asked him to throw a dart made out of mistletoe at Balder. Hother did as he was bade and the dart pierced Balder and killed him.

The heartbroken Frigga cried and cried until her tears turned into the white berries on the mistletoe. After begging the gods to bring her son back to life, Frigga's prayers were answered and her son was returned to her. An ecstatic Frigga stood beneath the mistletoe and kissed everyone who walked under it. After awhile, kissing under the mistletoe became a beloved custom, a celebration of love and peace.

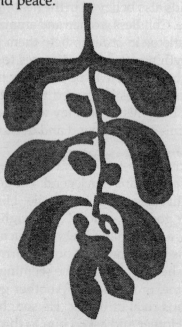

Poinsettia

This popular Christmas plant is named after Dr. Joel Roberts Poinsett, the United States' first ambassador to Mexico. Poinsett brought back the plant from his travels in our neighbor to the South in 1828. The Mexicans had been using the Poinsettia in their Christmas celebrations for hundreds of years. An early Mexican legend told of people who went to church in Cuernavaca on Christmas Eve to fill Christ's manger with flowers. When a poor boy could not find any flowers to bring to the church one year, an angel appeared and told him to pick some weeds from the side of the road. When the boy placed the weeds in the manger, they changed into Poinsettias. Because of its resemblance to the Star of Bethlehem, the Poinsettia is known as *Flor de la Noche Buena*, or the Flower of the Blessed Night, in Spanish.

Rosemary

Legend has it that rosemary gained its gray-green color from Mary's cloak, which she used to throw over its branches. Likewise, the sweet aroma of rosemary is said to have come from when Mary hung the baby Jesus's blankets over it. During the Middle Ages, people would place rosemary on their floors in order to keep their homes smelling nice. By the nineteenth century, rosemary was used to add flavor to the traditional Christmas dish of boar's head.

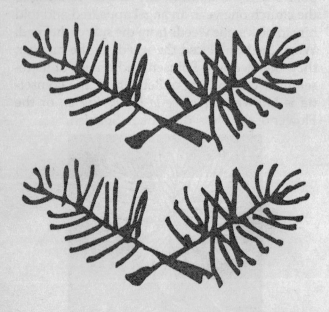

Rudolph, the Red-Nosed Reindeer

During the Christmas season of 1939, a Chicago branch of the Montgomery Ward department store handed out an illustrated poem to its customers. Robert May, an advertising copywriter, had created the story of a red-nosed reindeer who helped Santa see his way across the nighttime sky. 2.4 million copies of Rudolph were handed out that year, and the Rudolph legend became an indelible part of Christmas lore. In 1949, a friend of May's, Johnny Marks, put the poem to music. Gene Autry recorded the tune, which went on to become the second best-selling record of all-time (Bing Crosby's "White Christmas" is first).

Santa Claus

America's most beloved holiday figure has actually been created from a combination of many ancient legends. To begin with, in the fourth century, a bishop in the ancient Turkish town of Lycia (and later in the town of Myra, in Asia Minor) named Nicholas was famous for the way in which he watched over children, sailors and merchants. Legends sprang up about how he once brought three boys back to life. Another time he supposedly placed bags of gold down the chimney of three poor girls. He was also known to put a halt to storms at sea and to save sailors from shipwrecks. Indeed, the sight of Nicholas, with his long white beard, red-and-white biship's robe, and stubborn donkey, brought smiles to children and adults alike throughout Europe. Unfortunately, Nicholas was eventually imprisoned and tortured under orders of the Roman emperor Gaius Diocletianus. However, when Constantine replaced the despotic ruler, he freed Nicholas. After Nicholas died on December 6, 342, he was adopted as the patron saint of Russia, Greece, and Sicily.

In the eleventh century, a group of Italian merchants stole St. Nicholas' bones and moved them to Bari, Italy. People came from all over Europe to view the enormous tomb they erected, and by the end of the Middle Ages, hundreds of churches had been named after the kindly saint.

In the 16th century, during the Protestant Reformation, St. Nicholas was banned from most European countries. In his place, the secular figures of France's "Pape Noel," or England's "Father Christmas" appeared. However, the tradition of St. Nicholas remained alive and well in the Netherlands. Dutch children would refer to St. Nicholas as "Saint Nick." This gradually became "Sint Nikolass," and then "Sinterklass." When the Dutch arrived in America, the children pronounced his name "Santa Claus." Attempting to fit in with American culture, the Dutch decided to celebrate St. Nicholas Day on the same day as Christmas.

As far as Santa's home in the North Pole and reindeer and elves are concerned, the legend probably dates back thousands of years ago to a Northern European myth. The god Thor was thought to ride through the sky in a chariot pulled by reindeer. He would stop at people's homes for holiday feasts, and would travel with bearded elves or "tomtars," who would leave presents for children. However, much of the responsibility for these legends also falls on the shoulders of Dr. Clement Clarke Moore, who wrote "The Night Before Christmas" in 1822.

Likewise, Santa's appearance as a rosy-cheeked, rather corpulent man was created by another American, Thomas Nast. Nast's drawings of Santa in *Harper's Weekly* during the years 1863 to

1886 evolved from Dr. Moore's conception of a rather small, pudgy figure to the large, happy, bearded character that is so familiar today. Nast's images of Santa reading letters from children, building toys in his workshop, and closely monitoring children's behavior throughout the year have also become a significant part of Santa Claus lore.

Xmas

This popular abbreviation for Christmas apparently originated with the Greeks. X is the first letter of *Xristos*, the Greek word for Christ. By the 1500s, "Xmas" was in popular use throughout Europe.

"Yes, Virginia, There Is A Santa Claus"

In 1897, a little girl named Virginia O'Hanlon wrote a letter about the existence of Santa Claus to the New York Sun. A newspaper reporter named Francis Church wrote the now famous reply.

Dear Editor:

I am 8 years old. Some of my little friends say there is no Santa Claus. Papa says "If you see it in *The Sun* it's so." Please tell me the truth, is there a Santa Claus?

Virginia O'Hanlon,
115 West 95th Street

Reply:

Virginia, your little friends are wrong. They have been affected by the skepticism of a skeptical age. They do not believe except they see. They think that nothing can be which is not comprehensible by their little minds. All minds, Virginia, whether they be men's or children's, are little. In this great universe of ours man is a mere insect, an ant, in his intellect, as compared with the boundless world about him, as measured by the intelligence capable of grasping the whole of truth and knowledge.

Yes, Virginia, there is a Santa Claus. He exists as certainly as love and generosity and devotion exist, and you know that they abound and give to your life its highest beauty and joy. Alas! how dreary would be the world if there were no Santa Claus. It would be as dreary as if there were no Virginias. There would be no childlike faith then, no poetry, no romance to make tolerable this existence. We should have no enjoyment, except in sense and sight. The eternal light with which childhood fills the world would be extinguished.

Not believe in Santa Claus! You might as well not believe in fairies! You might get your papa to hire men to watch in all the chimneys on Christmas Eve to catch Santa Claus, but even if they did not see Santa Claus coming down, what would that prove? Nobody sees Santa Claus, but that is no sign that there is no Santa Claus. The most real things in the world are those that neither children nor men can see. Did you ever see fairies dancing on the lawn? Of course not, but that's no proof that they are not there. Nobody can conceive or imagine all the wonders there are unseen and unseeable in the world.

You may tear apart the baby's rattle and see what makes the noise inside, but there is a veil covering the unseen world which not the strongest man, nor even the united strength of all the strongest men that ever lived, could tear apart. Only faith, fancy, poetry, love, romance, can push aside that curtain and view and picture the supernal beauty and glory beyond. Is it all real? Ah,

Virginia, in all this world there is nothing else real and abiding.

No Santa Claus! Thank God he lives, and he lives forever. A thousand years from now, Virginia, nay, ten times ten thousand years from now, he will continue to make glad the heart of childhood.

Yule Log

The burning of the Yule Log dates back to the days before Christ was even born. People would burn the logs during the winter solstice in order to bring light, warmth, and hope during the darkest days of the year. The light of the log would help people have faith that spring was just around the corner, and that crops would grow plentiful once again. The flames from the log were also used to both scare away evil demons and spirits, and to provide warmth for the ghosts of ancestors.

In Scandinavia, the Yule log was set afire in honor of Thor, the god of thunder. Similarly, Europeans have longed believed that the Yule log helps protect their homes from thunder and lightning. The Germans especially believed in this particular power, as they would only burn the yule log for a short time during Christmas, reserving the rest of the log for days when thunderstorms broke out. In France, Yule logs were seen as helping animals become pregnant. After soaking the log in water, they would give the water to their cows to drink. The French also believed that there would be as many calves, goats, chickens and lambs as there were sparks in the Yule log.

Because we don't typically have fireplaces big enough to hold a Yule log, Americans tend to light a small fire in honor of this ancient Christmas tradition.

CHRISTMAS
CELEBRATIONS
AROUND
THE WORLD

Africa

Christmas is celebrated in many different ways throughout Africa. For instance, in Ghana, Christians send each other Christmas cards and decorate their homes with colorful flowers and green palm branches. Their version of Santa Claus is Father Christmas, who arrives out of the jungle bearing gifts for the children. On Christmas Eve, a great parade of children march through the streets singing, "*Egbona hee, egbona hee! Egogo vo,*" which means "Christ is coming! Christ is near!"

Meanwhile, in Ethiopia, Christians celebrate Christmas according to the Gregorian calendar—on January 7. Thousands of Christians make their way to the city of Lalibela for a special Christmas service conducted by a group of nuns, priests and monks. At the end of the day, a feast is held, where a great deal of eating, dancing, and sporting events take place.

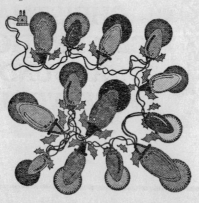

Britain

One of the most unique Christmas traditions in England is known as "mumming." This custom dates back to the Middle Ages, when people known as "mummers" would roam the countryside performing Christmas plays. These religiously-themed plays are still performed to this day throughout the country in everything from small villages to large cities.

December 26 is also a festive day in England. Known as Boxing Day, the citizens give presents to such public workers as the mailman or the newspaper boy. The name, "Boxing Day," originated when people would put money for the poor into boxes kept inside churches. On December 26, the priests would open up the boxes and give the money to the poor.

France

Christmas celebrations in France begin on Christmas Eve, when families set up their crèche. At midnight, church bells ring out, calling everyone to mass. After mass, the families return home for *Reveillon*, perhaps the grandest meal of the year. This magnificient feast usually features *pate de foie gras* and blood sausage. In many communities, children will wander through the streets singing Christmas carols while carrying a small crèche at the front of their procession.

Before going to bed on Christmas Eve, French children place their shoes in front of the fireplace, hoping that *Pere Noel* will fill them up with nuts and candy. It is usually not until New Year's Day that families exchange gifts. Children often arise early in the morning and greet their parents with gifts they have made and cheers of "*Bonne annee!*"

Finally, on Epiphany, *gateaux des rois*, or king's cakes, are baked in honor of the Magi. These round cakes are made with almond paste and feature a coin, bean or small gift inside. The child who finds the prize in his cake is given a paper crown and named king or queen for the day.

Germany

Because our Christmas tree, many of our carols, and such traditional Christmas recipes as gingerbread houses are originally from Germany, you can imagine that Germans celebrate Christmas much in the same manner as Americans. However, there are several differences. In many areas of Germany, for instance, citizens believe that Christ sends a messenger on Christmas Eve. This messenger appears in the form of an angel bearing gifts. The Germans call this angel, Christkind. Another popular German Christmas figure is *Weihnachtsmann* or "Christmas Man," who resembles our Santa Claus and who, like Santa, also brings gifts.

During Advent, which begins on the fourth Sunday before Christmas, Germans hang an Advent wreath with four candles. They then light one candle on each Sunday before Christmas. Great fairs, or *doms*, are held during these four weeks, during which town squares are filled with booths selling everything from fun-filled toys to luscious baked goods.

"Knocking Night" takes place on the Thursday before Christmas, when mummers in scary costumes go from house to house knocking on doors, cracking whips, and banging on cans and cowbells in an effort to drive away any evil spirits which may be lurking inside.

Italy

Interestingly, the Italians have a female version of Santa Claus known as "Lady *Befana*." *Befana* means "Epiphany." This beloved figure visits children on January 6 and leaves presents in their shoes if the children have been good during the previous year. If they've been bad, however, they will wake up to find a piece of coal in their shoes. An old legend claims that when Christ was born, the Magi asked *Befana* to bring them to Bethlehem. She refused, insisting that she was too busy sweeping the floors of her home. When she later realized what a fool she had been, she dedicated her life to roaming the earth, looking for the baby Jesus. Flying high in the air on her broomstick, she is thought to climb down the chimney to leave presents (or coal) for the children of Italy.

Italians love to build crèches or *precepios* in their homes, leaving them empty until Christmas Day when they place a baby or *bambino* in the structure. Surrounding the crèche is a *ceppo*, essentially a wooden pyramid with shelves. The top of the *ceppo* features a pine cone or a puppet, while wax candles are lit along the sides of the structure. At the very bottom, the infant Jesus lays in a cradle surrounded by shepherds, angels and saints. Candy, fruit and presents rest on the remainder of the shelves. The *ceppo* is essentially the Italian version of our Christmas tree, and some families even build one *ceppo* for each of their children.

An extremely colorful Italian custom is known as *pifferai*, or pipers. During Advent, shepherds dress up in sheepskin trousers, bright red vests and large hats with red tassels and white peacock feathers. They march from town to town carrying bagpipes and other instruments, playing music in front of churches and carpentry shops.

Japan

While only a very small portion of the Japanese are Christians, the Japanese still indulge in Christmas celebrations. Homes are decorated with evergreens and family and friends exchange gifts. A priest, known as *Hoteiosha*, even dresses up as Santa Claus and brings gifts to children.

Mexico

Mexicans celebrate for nine days before Christmas. These festive days are known as *posadas*. To begin with, on December 16, everyone places an empty manger, or *nacimiento*, on an altar in their home. For the next eight nights, friends and family gather together and act out the story of Mary and Joseph being turned away from the inn at Bethlehem. When the play ends, children take turns trying to break open a *pinata*—a paper or clay jug decorated gaily and filled with candy and other surprises. Then, on the ninth night, or Christmas Eve, the holy pilgrims are welcomed inside. The family will decorate the altar with flowers and tinsel, and then place a baby Jesus in the manger. Christ's birth is marked by a celebration featuring singing, dancing and feasting until the Mass of the Cock or *Missa da Gallo*. Finally, on Epiphany Eve, children place their shoes in the window of their homes in the hope that the Magi will leave gifts as they pass by during the night.

Russia

Prior to the Russian Revolution of 1917, the Russian people celebrated the Christmas season with great gusto. They had mumming parades, sang songs, and exchanged gifts. The end of the Christmas season was marked by Epiphany Eve, when *Babushka*, a female figure bearing gifts, left presents for the children.

However, after the Russian Revolution, Christmas was banned by authorities. Today, the Russians have combined many aspects of our Christmas celebration with those of New Year's Day. They have a New Year's tree which they decorate, and Russian children dress up in costumes while waiting for *Dyet Moroz* or "Grandfather Frost" and *Syyegorochka* or "The Snow Maiden" to bring them gifts.

Spain

The Christmas season in Spain begins on December 8, which is the Feast of the Immaculate Conception. The regal Dance of the Sixes is performed on this day, during which boys dressed in plumed hats and blue satin suits dance intricate steps to the clickety-clack sound of the castanets.

Throughout the holidays, families gather around Nacimientos, or manger scenes, and sing songs, dance, and celebrate the Christmas season.

Special holiday foods, such as dulces de almendra, or sweet almond pastry, are served, and a good time is had by all.

One of the most unique Christmas traditions of the Spanish is that of the Urn of Fate. After attending church on Christmas day, the members of a village will gather in the town square for an evening of dancing, singing and eating. During this festive night, everyone places their name in the Urn of Fate. Two names at a time are then drawn, and the matched pair are then said to be fated to become best friends during the forthcoming year.

Another fascinating custom is "swinging the sun." This ancient rite is performed by children, who set up swings in the public squares and see who can go the highest in the air to help the sun begin its long journey towards the north.

On January 6, Spanish children eagerly await the coming of the Three Kings from the East— Gaspar, Melchoir, and Balthasar—who travel across the countryside bringing gifts for boys and girls who have behaved well during the year. Before they go to sleep, the children place straw in their shoes and set them on windowsills, balconies and doorways so that the Kings' horses will have plenty to eat during their journey. In the morning, the children awake to find the straw replaced with candy and gifts.

Sweden

The official beginning of Christmas in Sweden is St. Lucia's Day, which falls on December 13. Lucia was a girl who grew up in Sicily during the fourth century. While it was against the law at the time to believe in Christ, Lucia was, nevertheless, a fervent believer. When a man who did not believe in Christ asked her to marry him, she refused. The man was so upset that he complained to the governor, who in turn had the girl murdered. Two centuries later, Lucia was made a saint.

How did a Sicilian girl become such a popular figure in Sweden? Nobody knows for certain. One legend claims that Lucia appeared to the Swedish people during a winter famine with food for everyone. Whatever the reason for the Swede's fascination with Lucia, there are certain traditions honoring the Saint which are observed year after year. Early in the morning on December 13, the eldest daughter in a family dresses up in a white robe and silver belt and places a crown of lingonberry leaves and twelve lighted candles on her head. She then wakes up everyone in the household with hot coffee and pastries. Every town also has an official St. Lucia, and the lucky girl chosen to represent her leads a parade through the town.

On Christmas Eve, the people of Sweden look forward to the arrival of *Jultomtem*, a gnome who swoops down in a sleigh pulled by a goat. After everyone has retired for the evening, *Jultomtem* leaves presents for people and food for animals. The Swedes themselves make certain that animals are not forgotten by giving them extra rations. Birds, too, are taken care of by means of a sheaf of wheat that is dipped in cooking fat and then mounted on a large pole above the snow.

Julkapp is another popular custom whereby a person knocks on a friend's door and, when the door is opened, he or she tosses a present into the house and runs away. The present is usually wrapped in many, many layers of paper.

Ten days after Christmas, the Swedes celebrate Epiphany Eve, during which young boys dress up as the Magi, sing Christmas carols, and carry stars on poles through the streets. They are often referred to as the "Star Boys," and their ritual is essentially a reenactment of the journey of the Three Kings to Bethlehem. During their parade about town, they are followed by costumed figures, such as Judas with his purse. Finally, on January 13, the Swedes celebrate the end of the Christmas season with St. Knut's Day. King Knut IV was an ancient ruler who deemed that Christmas end twenty days after Christmas Day. So on St. Knut's Day, the Swedes take down their Christmas trees and sing, "The twentieth day, King Knut did rule / Would end the festival of Yule."

CHRISTMAS
STORIES

The Fir Tree
Hans Christian Anderson (1805-1875)

Out in the forest stood a pretty little Fir Tree. It had a good place; it could have sunlight, air there was in plenty, and all around grew many larger comrades—pines as well as firs. But the little Fir Tree wished ardently to become greater. It did not care for the warm sun and the fresh air; it took no notice of the peasant children, who went about talking together, when they had come out to look for strawberries and raspberries. Often they came with a whole potful, or had strung berries on a straw; then they would sit down by the little Fir Tree and say, "How pretty and small that one is!" and the Fir Tree did not like to hear that at all.

Next year he had grown a great joint, and the following year he was longer still, for in fir trees one can always tell by the number of rings they have how many years they have been growing.

"Oh, if I were only as great a tree as the others!" sighed the little Fir, "then I would spread my branches far around and look out from my crown into the wide world. The birds would then build nests in my boughs, and when the wind blew I could nod just as grandly as the others yonder."

He took no pleasure in the sunshine, in the birds, and in the red clouds that went sailing over him morning and evening.

When it was winter, the snow lay all around,

white and sparkling, a hare would often come jumping along, and spring right over the little Fir Tree. Oh! this made him so angry. But two winters went by, and when the third came the little Tree had grown so tall that the hare was obliged to run around it.

"Oh! to grow, to grow, and become old; that's the only fine thing in the world," thought the Tree.

In the autumn woodcutters always came and felled a few of the largest trees; that was done this year too, and the little Fir Tree, that was now quite well grown, shuddered with fear, for the great stately trees fell to the ground with a crash, and their branches were cut off, so that the trees looked quite naked, long, and slender—they could hardly be recognized. But then they were laid upon wagons, and horses dragged them away out of the wood. Where were they going? What destiny awaited them?

In the spring when the Swallows and the Stork came, the tree asked them, "Do you know where they were taken? Did you not meet them?"

The Swallows knew nothing about it, but the Stork looked thoughtful, nodded his head, and said:

"Yes, I think so. I met many new ships when I flew out of Egypt; on the ships were stately masts; I fancy these were the trees. They smelled like fir. I can assure you they're stately—very stately."

"Oh that I were only big enough to go over the

sea! What kind of thing is this sea, and how does it look?"

"It would take too long to explain all that," said the Stork, and he went away.

"Rejoice in thy youth," said the Sunbeams; "rejoice in thy fresh growth, and in the young life that is within thee."

And the wind kissed the Tree, and the dew wept tears upon it; but the Fir Tree did not understand about that.

When Christmas time approached, quite young trees were felled, sometimes trees which were neither so old nor so large as this Fir Tree, that never rested, but always wanted to go away. These young trees, which were always the most beautiful, kept all their branches; they were put upon wagons, and the horses dragged them away out of the wood.

"Where are they all going?" asked the Fir Tree. "They are not greater than I—indeed, one of them was much smaller. Why do they keep all their branches? Whither are they taken?"

"We know that! We know that!" chirped the Sparrows. "Yonder in the town we looked in at the window. We know where they go. Oh! they are dressed up in the greatest pomp and splendor that can be imagined. We have looked in at the windows, and have perceived that they are planted in the middle of a warm room, and adorned with the most beautiful things—gilt apples, honey cakes, playthings, and many hundreds of candles."

"And then?" asked the Fir Tree, and trembled through all its branches. "And then? What happens then?"

"Why, we have not seen anything more. But it is incomparable."

"Perhaps I may be destined to tread this glorious path one day!" cried the Fir Tree, rejoicingly. "That is even better than traveling across the sea. How painfully I long for it! If it were only Christmas now! Now I am great and grown, up, like the rest who were led away last year. Oh, if I were only on the carriage! If I were only in the warm room, among all the pomp and splendor! And then? Yes, then something even better will come, something far more charming, or else why should they adorn me so? There must be something grander, something greater still to come; but what? Oh! I'm suffering. I'm longing! I don't know myself what is the matter with me!"

"Rejoice in us," said the Air and Sunshine. "Rejoice in thy fresh youth here in the woodland."

But the Fir Tree did not rejoice at all, but it grew and grew; winter and summer it stood there, green, dark green. The people who saw it said, "That's a handsome tree!" and at Christmas time it was felled before any of the others. The ax cut deep into its marrow, and the tree fell to the ground with a sigh; it felt a pain, a sensation of faintness, and could not think at all of happiness, for it was sad at parting from its home, from the place where it had grown up; it knew that it should never again see the dear old companions, the little bushes and flowers all around—perhaps not even the birds. The parting was not at all agreeable.

The Tree only came to itself when it was un-loaded in a yard, with other trees, and heard a man say:

"This one is famous; we want only this one!"

Now two servants came in gay liveries, and carried the Fir Tree into a large, beautiful salon. All around the walls hung pictures, and by the great stove stood large Chinese vases with lions on the covers; there were rocking-chairs, silken sofas, great tables covered with picture-books, and toys worth a hundred times a hundred dollars, at least the children said so. And the Fir Tree was put into a great tub filled with sand; but no one could see that it was a tub, for it was hung round with green cloth, and stood on a large, many-colored carpet. Oh, how the Tree trembled! What was to happen now? The servants, and the young ladies also, decked it out. On one branch they hung little nets, cut out of colored paper; every net was filled with sweetmeats; golden apples and walnuts hung down, as if they grew there, and more than a hundred little candles, red, white, and blue, were fastened to the different boughs. Dolls that looked exactly like real people—the Tree had never seen such before—swung among the foliage, and high on the summit of the Tree was fixed a tinsel star. It was splendid, particularly splendid.

"This evening," said all, "this evening it will shine."

"Oh," thought the Tree, "that it were evening already! Oh, that the lights may soon be lit up! When may that be done? Will the sparrows fly against the panes? Shall I grow fast here, and stand adorned in summer and winter?"

Yes, he did not guess badly. But he had a complete backache from mere longing, and backache is just as bad for a tree as a headache for a person.

At last the candles were lighted. What a brilliance, what a splendor! The Tree trembled so in all its branches that one of the candles set fire to a green twig, and it was scorched.

"Heaven preserve us!" cried the young ladies; and they hastily put the fire out.

Now the Tree might not even tremble. Oh, that was terrible! It was so afraid of setting fire to some of its ornaments, and it was quite bewildered with all the brilliance. And now the folding doors were thrown wide open, and a number of children rushed in as if they would have overturned the whole Tree; the older people followed more deliberately. The little ones stood quite silent, but only for a minute; they then shouted till the room rang; they danced gleefully round the Tree, and one present after another was plucked from it.

"What are they about?" thought the Tree. "What's going to be done?"

And the candles burned down to the twigs, and as they burned down they were extinguished, and then the children received permission to plunder the Tree. Oh! they rushed in upon it, so that every branched cracked again; if it had not been fastened by the top and by the golden star to the ceiling, it would have fallen down.

The children danced about with their pretty toys. No one looked at the Tree except one old man, who came up and peeped among the branches, but only to see if a fig or an apple had not been forgotten.

"A story! A story!" shouted the children; and they drew a little fat man toward the Tree; and he sat down just beneath—"for then we shall be in the green wood," said he, "and the tree may have the advantage of listening to my tale. But I can only tell one. Will you hear the story of Ivede-Avede, or of Klumpey-Dumpey, who fell downstairs, and still was raised up to honor and married the Princess?"

"Ivede-Avede!" cried some. "Klumpey-Dumpey!" cried others, and there was a great crying and shouting. Only the Fir Tree was quite silent, and thought, "Shall I not be in it? Shall I have nothing to do in it?" But he had been in the evening's amusement, and had done what was required of him.

And the fat man told about Klumpey-Dumpey who fell downstairs and yet was raised to honor and married a Princess. And the children clapped their hands and cried, "Tell another! tell another!" and they wanted to hear about Ivede-Avede; but they only got the story of Klumpey-Dumpey. The Fir Tree stood quite silent and thoughtful; never had the birds in the wood told such a story as that. Klumpey-Dumpey fell downstairs, and yet came to honor and married a Princess!

"Yes, so it happens in the world!" thought the Fir Tree, and believed it must be true, because that was such a nice man who told it.

"Well, who can know? Perhaps I shall fall downstairs, too, and marry a Princess!" And it looked forward with pleasure to being adorned again, the next evening, with candles and toys, gold and fruit. "Tomorrow I shall not tremble," it thought.

"I shall rejoice in all my splendor. Tomorrow I shall hear the story of Klumpey-Dumpey again, and perhaps that of Ivede-Avede, too."

And the Tree stood all night quiet and thoughtful.

In the morning the servants and the chambermaid came in.

"Now my splendor will begin afresh," thought the Tree. But they dragged him out of the room, and upstairs to the garret, and here they put him in a dark corner where no daylight shone.

"What's the meaning of this?" thought the Tree.

113

"What am I to do here? What is to happen?"

And he leaned against the wall, and thought, and thought. And he had time enough, for days and nights went by, and nobody came up; and when at length someone came, it was only to put some great boxes in a corner. Now the Tree stood quite hidden away, and the supposition is that it was quite forgotten.

"Now it's winter outside," thought the Tree. "The earth is hard and covered with snow, and people cannot plant me; therefore I supposed I'm to be sheltered here until Spring comes. How considerate that is! How good people are! If it were only not so dark in here, and so terribly solitary! Not even a little hare? That was pretty out there in the wood, when the snow lay thick and the hare sprang past; yes, even when he jumped over me; but then I did not like it. It is terribly lonely up here!"

"Piep! piep!" said a little Mouse, and crept forward, and then came another little one. They smelled at the Fir Tree, and then slipped among the branches.

"It's horribly cold," said the two little Mice, "or else it would be comfortable here. Don't you think so, old Fir Tree?"

"I'm not old at all," said the Fir Tree. "There are many much older than I."

"Where do you come from?" asked the Mice. "And what do you know?" They were dreadfully inquisitive. "Tell us about the most beautiful spot on earth. Have you been there? Have you been in the storeroom, where cheeses lie on the shelves, and hams hang from the ceiling, where one dances on tallow candles, and goes in thin and comes out fat?"

"I don't know that," replied the Tree; "but I know the wood, where the sun shines and the birds sing."

And then it told all about its youth.

And the little Mice had never heard anything of the kind; and they listened and said:

"What a number of things you have seen! How happy you must have been!"

"I?" replied the Fir Tree; and it thought about what it had told. "Yes, those were really quite happy times." But then he told of the Christmas Day, when he had been hung with sweetmeats and candles.

"Oh!" said the little Mice, "how happy you have been, you old Fir Tree!"

"I'm not old at all," said the Tree. "I only came out of the wood this winter. I'm only rather backward in my growth."

"What splendid stories you can tell!" said the little Mice.

And the next night they came with four other little Mice, to hear what the Tree had to relate; and the more it said, the more clearly did it remember everything, and thought, "Those were quite merry days! But they may come again. Klumpey-Dumpey fell downstairs, and yet he married a Princess. Perhaps I shall marry a Princess, too!" And the Fir Tree thought of a pretty little Birch Tree that grew out in the forest; for the Fir Tree, that Birch was a real Princess.

"Who's Klumpey-Dumpey?" asked the little Mice.

And then the Fir Tree told the whole story. It could remember every single word; and the little Mice were ready to leap to the very top of the Tree with pleasure. Next night a great many more Mice came, and on Sunday two Rats even appeared; but these thought the story was not pretty, and the little Mice were sorry for that, for now they also did not like it so much as before.

"Do you know only one story?" asked the Rats.

"Only that one," replied the Tree. "I heard that on the happiest evening of my life; I did not think then how happy I was."

"That's a very miserable story. Don't you know any about bacon and tallow candles—a storeroom story?"

"No," said the Tree.

"Then we'd rather not hear you," said the Rats.

And they went back to their own people. The little Mice at last stayed away also; and then the Tree sighed and said:

"It was very nice when they sat round me, the merry little Mice, and listened when I spoke to them. Now that's past too. But I shall remember to be pleased when they take me out."

But when did that happen? Why, it was one morning that people came and rummaged in the garret; the boxes were put away, and the Tree brought out; they certainly threw him rather roughly on the floor, but a servant dragged him away at once to the stairs, where the daylight shone.

"Now life is beginning again!" thought the Tree.

It felt the fresh air and the first sunbeam, and now it was out in the courtyard. Everything passed so quickly that the Tree quite forgot to look at itself, there was so much to look at all round. The courtyard was close to a garden, and here everything was blooming; the roses hung fresh over the paling, the linden trees were in blossom, and the swallows cried, "Quinze-wit! quinze-wit! my husband's come!" But it was not the Fir Tree they meant.

"Now I shall live!" said the Tree, rejoicingly, and spread its branches far out; but, alas! they were all withered and yellow; and it lay in the corner among nettles and weeds. The tinsel star was still upon it, and shone in the bright sunshine.

In the courtyard a couple of the merry children were playing who had danced round the Tree at Christmas time, and had rejoiced over it. One of the youngest ran up and tore off the golden star.

"Look what is sticking to the ugly old fir tree!"

said the child, and he trod upon the branches till thy cracked again under his boots.

And the Tree looked at all the blooming flowers and the splendor of the garden, and then looked at itself, and wished it had remained in the dark corner of the garret; it thought of its fresh youth in the wood, of the merry Christmas Eve, and of the little Mice which had listened so pleasantly to the story of Klumpey-Dumpey.

"Past! past!" said the old Tree. "Had I but rejoiced when I could have done so! Past! past!"

And the servant came and chopped the Tree into little pieces; a whole bundle lay there; it blazed brightly under the great brewing copper, and it sighed deeply, and each sigh was like a little shot; and the children who were at play there ran up and seated themselves at the fire, looked into it, and cried "Puff! puff!" But at each explosion, which was a deep sigh, the Tree thought of a summer day in the woods, or of a winter night there, when the stars beamed; he thought of Christmas Eve and of Klumpey-Dumpey, the only story he had ever heard or knew how to tell; and then the Tree was burned.

The boys played in the garden, and the youngest had on his breast a golden star, which the Tree had worn on its happiest evening. Now that was past, and the Tree's life was past, and the story is past too: past! past!—and that's the way with all stories.

The Gift Of The Magi
O. Henry (1862-1910)

One dollar and eighty-seven cents. That was all. And sixty cents of it was in pennies. Pennies saved one and two at a time by bulldozing the grocer and the vegetable man and the butcher until one's cheeks burned with the silent imputation of parsimony that such close dealing implied. Three times Della counted it. One dollar and eighty-seven cents. And the next day would be Christmas.

There was clearly nothing to do but flop down on the shabby little couch and howl. So Della did it. Which instigates the moral reflection that life is made up of sobs, sniffles, and smiles, with sniffles predominating.

While the mistress of the home is gradually subsiding from the first stage to the second, take a look at the home. A furnished flat at $8 per week. It did not exactly beggar description, but it certainly had that word on the lookout for the mendicancy squad.

In the vestibule below was a letter box into which no mortal finger could coax a ring. Also appertaining thereunto was a card bearing the name "Mr. James Dillingham Young."

The "Dillingham" had been flung to the breeze during a former period of prosperity when its possessor was being paid $30 per week. Now, when the income was shrunk to $20, the letters of "Dillingham" looked blurred, as though they were thinking seriously of contracting to a modest and unassuming D. But whenever Mr. James Dillingham Young came home and reached his flat above he was called "Jim" and greatly hugged by Mrs. James Dillingham Young, already introduced to you as Della. Which is all very good.

Della finished her cry and attended to her cheeks with the powder rag. She stood by the window and looked out dully at a gray cat walking a gray fence in a gray backyard. Tomorrow would be Christmas Day and she had only $1.87 with which to buy Jim a present. She had been saving every penny she could for months, with this result. Twenty dollars a week doesn't go far. Expenses had been greater than she had calculated. They always are. Only $1.87 to buy a present for Jim. Her Jim. Many a happy hour she had spent planning for something nice for him. Something fine and rare and sterling—something just a little bit near to being worthy of the honor of being owned by Jim.

There was a pier glass between the windows of the room. Perhaps you have seen a pier glass in an $8 flat. A very thin and very agile person may, by observing his reflection in a rapid sequence of longitudinal strips, obtain a fairly accurate conception of his looks. Della, being slender, had mastered the art.

Suddenly she whirled from the window and stood before the glass. Her eyes were shining brilliantly, but her face had lost its color within twenty seconds. Rapidly she pulled down her hair and let it fall to its full length.

Now, there were two possessions of the James Dillingham Youngs in which they both took a mighty pride. One was Jim's gold watch that had been his father's and his grandfather's. The other was Della's hair. Had the Queen of Sheba lived in the flat across the airshaft, Della would have let her hair hang out the window someday to dry just to depreciate Her Majesty's jewels and gifts. Had King Solomon been the janitor, with all his treasures piled up in the basement, Jim would have pulled out his watch every time he passed, just to see him pluck at his beard from envy.

So now Della's beautiful hair fell about her, rippling and shining like a cascade of brown waters. It reached below her knee and made itself almost a garment for her. And then she did it up again nervously and quickly. Once she faltered for a minute and stood still while a tear or two splashed on the worn red carpet.

On went her old brown jacket; on went her old brown hat. With a whirl of skirts and with the brilliant sparkle still in her eyes, she fluttered out the door and down the stairs to the street.

Where she stopped the sign read: "Mme.. Sofronie. Hair Goods of All Kinds." One flight up

Della ran, and collected herself, panting. Madame, large, too white, chilly, hardly looked the "Sofronie."

"Will you buy my hair?" asked Della.

"I buy hair," said Madame. "Take yer hat off and let's have a sight at the looks of it."

Down rippled the brown cascade.

"Twenty dollars," said Madame, lifting the mass with a practiced hand.

"Give it to me quick," said Della.

Oh, and the next two hours tripped by on rosy wings. Forget the hashed metaphor. She was ransacking the stores for Jim's present.

She found it at last. It surely had been made for Jim and no one else. There was no other like it in any of the stores, and she had turned all of them inside out. It was a platinum fob chain simple and chaste in design, properly proclaiming its value by substance alone and not by meretricious ornamentation—as all good things should do. It was even worthy of The Watch. As soon as she saw it she knew that it must be Jim's. It was like him. Quietness and value—the description applied to both. Twenty-one dollars they took from her for it, and she hurried home with the 87 cents. With that chain on his watch Jim might be properly anxious about the time in any company. Grand as the watch was, he sometimes looked at it on the sly on account of the old leather strap that he used in place of a chain.

When Della reached home her intoxication gave way a little to prudence and reason. She got out her curling irons and lighted the gas and went to work repairing the ravages made by generosity added to love. Which is always a tremendous task, dear friends—a mammoth task.

Within forty minutes her head was covered with tiny, close-lying curls that made her look wonderfully like a truant schoolboy. She looked at her reflection in the mirror long, carefully, and critically.

"If Jim doesn't kill me," she said to herself, "before he takes a second look at me, he'll say I look like a Coney Island chorus girl. But what could I do—oh! what could I do with a dollar and eighty-seven cents?"

At 7 o'clock the coffee was made and the frying pan was on the back of the stove hot and ready to cook the chips.

Jim was never late. Della doubled the fob chain in her hand and sat on the corner of the table near the door that he always entered. Then she heard his step on the stair away down on the first flight, and she turned white for just a moment. She had a habit of saying little silent prayers about the simplest everyday things, and now she whispered: "Please God, make him think I am still pretty."

The door opened and Jim stepped in and closed it. He looked thin and very serious. Poor fellow, he was only twenty-two—and to be burdened with a family! He needed a new overcoat and he was without gloves.

Jim stepped inside the door, as immovable as a setter at the scent of quail. His eyes were fixed upon Della, and there was an expression in them that she could not read, and it terrified her. It was not anger, not surprise, nor disapproval, nor horror, nor any of the sentiments that she had been prepared for. He simply stared at her fixedly with that peculiar expression on his face.

Della wriggled off the table and went for him.

"Jim, darling," she cried, "don't look at me that way. I had my hair cut off and sold it because I couldn't have lived through Christmas without giving you a present. It'll grow out again—you won't mind, will you? I just had to do it. My hair grows awfully fast. Say 'Merry Christmas!' Jim, and let's be happy. You don't know what a nice—what a beautiful, nice gift I've got for you."

"You've cut off your hair?" asked Jim, laboriously, as if he had not arrived at that patent fact yet even after the hardest mental labor.

"Cut it off and sold it," said Della. "Don't you like me just as well, anyhow? I'm me without my hair, ain't I?"

Jim looked about the room curiously.

"You say your hair is gone?" he said, with an air almost of idiocy.

"You needn't look for it," said Della. "It's sold, I tell you—sold and gone, too. It's Christmas Eve, boy. Be good to me, for it went for you. Maybe the hairs on my head were numbered," she went on with a sudden serious sweetness, "but nobody could ever count my love for you. Shall I put the chops on, Jim?"

Out of his trance Jim seemed quickly to wake. He enfolded his Della. For ten seconds let us regard with discreet scrutiny some inconsequential object in the other direction. Eight dollars a week or a million a year—what is the difference? A mathematician or a wit would give you the wrong answer. The magi brought valuable gifts, but that was not among them. This dark assertion will be illuminated later on.

Jim drew a package from his overcoat pocket and threw it upon the table.

"Don't make any mistake, Dell," he said, "about me. I don't think there's anything in the way of a haircut or a shave or a shampoo that could make me like my girl any less. But if you'll unwrap that package you may see why you had me going a while at first."

White fingers and nimble tore at the string and paper. And then an ecstatic scream of joy; and then, alas! a quick feminine change to hysterical tears and wails, necessitating the immediate employment of all the comforting powers of the lord of the flat.

For there lay The Combs—the set of combs, side and back, that Della had worshipped for long in

a Broadway window. Beautiful combs, pure tor-
toiseshell, with jeweled rims—just the shade to
wear in the beautiful vanished hair. They were
expensive combs, she knew, and her heart had
simply craved and yearned over them without
the least hope of possession. And now, they were
hers, but the tresses that should have adorned the
coveted adornments were gone.

But she hugged them to her bosom, and at
length she was able to look up with dim eyes and
a smile and say: "My hair grows so fast, Jim!"

And then Della leaped up like a little singed cat
and cried, "Oh, oh!"

Jim had not yet seen his beautiful present. She
held it out to him eagerly upon her open palm.
The dull precious metal seemed to flash with a
reflection of her bright and ardent spirit.

"Isn't it a dandy, Jim? I hunted all over town to
find it. You'll have to look at the time a hundred
times a day now. Give me your watch. I want to
see how it looks on it."

Instead of obeying, Jim tumbled down on the
couch and put his hands under the back of his
head and smiled.

"Dell," said he, "let's put our Christmas presents away and keep 'em a while. They're too nice
to use just at present. I sold the watch to get the
money to buy your combs. And now suppose you
put the chops on."

The magi, as you know, were wise men—wonderfully wise men—who brought gifts to the Babe in the manger. They invented the art of giving Christmas presents. Being wise, their gifts were no doubt wise ones, possibly bearing the privilege of exchange in case of duplication. And here I have lamely related to you the uneventful chronicle of two foolish children in a flat who most unwisely sacrificed for each other the greatest treasures of their house. But in a last word to the wise of these days let it be said that of all who give gifts these two were the wisest. Of all who give and receive gifts, such as they are wisest. Everywhere they are wisest. They are the magi.